Keep Control and Self-Publish:
Simple Steps To Self-Publish Your First Book

NONNAC CONTENT & PRESS

For information: AuthorS.W.Cannon@gmail.com

www.AuthorSWCannon.com

ISBN- 978-0-9895183-2-1

1. Non-Fiction 2. Self-Help 3. How-To 4. Guide 5. Blue Print

Cover Design by S. W. Cannon with photography by D. Jerome Smedley

Dedication

I dedicate this book to all of the indie writers before me. Thanks to your bravery and the beaten path you left for me to follow, I am able to share these very important steps to freedom with soon-to-be first-time authors everywhere. I hope to make you proud, as I widen my reach to increase your legacy.

Acknowledgements

I acknowledge my family for making the sacrifice of my time as I worked on my passion of helping authors.

I acknowledge the never-ending support of my book club In The Company Of Twelve (ITC12) in Birmingham, Alabama. Even when I showed up to meetings without having read that month's book, they were understanding and supportive of my big picture.

I acknowledge Tasha "TC" Cooper of Upward Action® (**www.UpwardActionMedia.com**) and Dr. Will Moreland (**www.WillMoreland.com**) for being two of the greatest word-of-mouth advertisers for my self-publishing services.

The Case For Self-Publishing

The advantage of a publishing house/firm is that they do most of the post writing work. The two huge provisions they supply are legal protection and big budget marketing. An author not having to come out of pocket for professional services, is another advantage of a publisher. Rejection is high because publishers are not willing to take a chance on most new authors. Although you can submit to a publishing company directly, you usually have to involve a literary agent to be considered by them. Literary agents are the gate keepers to the publishing companies for unknown writers, much like casting agents are the gate keeper to big studio movies for unknown actors and actresses. This is a huge con as it is yet another piece of the profit pie you'll have to share.

Something to think about: success to a publishing company that fronts the money for your book to be published is approximately 3,000 to 5,000 books sold. However, the average number of books sold by an unknown author is around 250 to 300 books. That total represents books sold across all formats (print, ebook and audio) over the lifetime of the book. That means books sold EVER, not just the first few years. As you can imagine not many books that make it to publication with a larger publisher actually makes a profit for the publisher.

The biggest con to utilizing the publishing company route is the lack of control over your work: final edits, cover art, marketing budget, marketing choices, and sometimes even the subject matter or focus of your entire book. To boot, did you know a publisher can obtain the rights to your book and decide if that book will be published to the public at all?

I won't even beat around the bush on this one. I am a huge proponent of self-publishing. Call me a control freak but I want to have the last word on how my book cover will look, what my content is about, what will get edited out of my content, how my book will be marketed, etc... Publishing your work is the alternative to those problems, but it's no picnic either. You have the control but you also have the responsibility of everything necessary for publication: copyrighting, legalities, marketing and all out of pocket expenses.

I won't lie to you; when I made the decision to self-publish my very first book, I was afraid. I was afraid that my book wasn't as good as I thought and there would be no one to tell me. I was afraid that I couldn't sell as many copies without the help of a well-known publishing house. But even more terrifying to me than these things was handing over control of all that was important to me regarding this baby I'd breathed life into. Like a parent, I wanted to be responsible for raising it the way I saw fit.

Be careful of some of the publishers out there. I've heard horror stories about authors allowing so-called publishers to publish their books. A fellow author and friend of mine allowed one of these 'publishers' to distribute his book on Amazon as a print book and a Kindle ebook. He gave them his final draft and they 'published' it on Amazon. He was happy with the result. Then he started realizing he wasn't getting paid from confirmed sales. When the 'publishing company' stopped being responsive, he also realized there was no way to gain control over the money that came in from Amazon. To add insult to injury, he also did not have control over the price set for the book nor the ability to change the price of the book, make any corrections to the version currently on sale or obtain printed copies of his book at the wholesale price at will.

THE SOLUTION: Pay to have your book formatted for Amazon print and ebook, then submit it for distribution under an Amazon account that you control over. There are no upfront costs to uploading your formatted book and cover art to Amazon for distribution. Much like PayPal, they take a certain amount per book transaction and send you the balance. You can even purchase printed copies of your book at a wholesale price (the cost of printing only, instead of the retail price of your book). The more books you purchase, the less your total wholesale cost for the books.

Horror story number two came from an author I met at a book fair. He displayed and sold his books right next to my booth. Being so close in proximity, we began a conversation. He revealed he paid $3800 for a 'publishing company' to 'publish' his book for distribution on Amazon as a print book only. Within his $3800 package, he was to receive Amazon distribution, 200 printed copies of his book, and a website to promote his book. On the day we attended the book fair, it had been a year since he paid for his package and he still didn't have a website. He also didn't have direct control over his Amazon account to track sales, monitor analytics, and make changes to the book or the price.

THE SOLUTION: Once again, pay to have your book formatted for Amazon print and submitted for distribution under an Amazon account that YOU control. Pay to receive printed copies of your book in quantities according to your budget or pending opportunities to sell your book inventory. Pay for a simple website. Had he done these things using a la carte services, for the size and format of his book his out of pocket expense would have been well under half of what he paid in total.

I believe an author should be able to control the destiny of their talent. I believe in self-publishing. The so-called 'publishers' play the middle man, which increases the price of the same a la carte services you can easily get access to AND they keep control of your hard work. The hardest part of the publishing process for a self-publisher is marketing the book to unconnected readers and attaining legal protection. These services can be invested in a la carte. Both of these services are usually what the so-called 'publishing companies' lack in offering also. This is a huge indicator that you are not dealing with a 'real' publisher. Instead, they are the middle man increasing the price of the same a la carte services an author can easily have access to while they keep control of your hard work.

The Self- Publishing Steps

You've written your full first book draft, now what?

1. **Author Platform**
2. **Beta-Readers**
3. **Legalities**
4. **Editing**
5. **Formatting**
6. **Book Cover**
7. **ISBN**
8. **PCN**
9. **Genre Assignment**
10. **Copyright**
11. **POD**
12. **Marketing**

Be sure to read this book in its entirety. Do NOT set a book launch date until you have considered each step from 1-11. Decisions within those steps can directly impact your actual date of publication.

Author Platform

Most people believe the marketing of a book starts <u>after</u> the book is written and printed. The truth is, your journey in marketing should begin <u>before</u> you start to write. Building an AUTHOR PLATFORM should be your first step. Unless you have a publishing company willing to spend a big budget on marketing for your book once it is published, you have to begin to create buzz about your book now. What is an author platform? The word *platform* means a raised level surface on which people or things can stand. As an author, you need to be raised where your readers can see you. Rise by nurturing awareness of your book, while building a relationship with your target readers now.

Social Media is definitely the great equalizer

between self-publishers, small publishers, and large, well-known publishing houses. It doesn't take a marketing genius to cultivate social media and create what I call a *Google Footprint*. This footprint is created when your web presence as an author comes up in the Google search listing for your name. The more places your name as an author can be found on the internet, the larger your Google Footprint will become.

Let's grow your footprint:

- create a Facebook account for your author name;
- create a Twitter account for your author name;
- create a LinkedIn account for your author name; and
- create an author website.

If you already have some of the social media accounts listed, you may change the account names to your author name or by simply adding the title author in front of your name. BUT, ask yourself if your current followers are your target readers. It's best to start a new account and attract your target readers so that your attempts to connect are not in vain.

This may seem like a lot to maintain, however there is technology that can help you automate content for some of these accounts. Hootsuite and Dynamic Tweets are two such technologies available at the time of publication for this book. A few of these accounts will not require any or little maintenance once fully created. Another way to increase your platform is to register with Good Reads for an author profile. Then go a step further and add a few original quotes to the Good Reads site. If you are not camera shy, consider the following to add to your arsenal: Periscope account, Meerkat account, Blab account, and/or a YouTube Channel.

How are you using all of these outlets? Start talking about your book. Take your followers on the journey with you while you are writing the book. Introduce your followers to your characters, tips or steps. Create a rapport that will lead to a pool of ready-made potential readers for your book upon completion.

The most natural thing you can do to get the word out about your book is to speak up. Whenever the opportunity arises, appropriately share that you are writing a book, what it will be about and how anyone interested can obtain a copy in the format of their choice once you are done.

If you would like more information on building your author platform, please connect with me at **www.AuthorSWCannon.com/connect**.

What Do You Think

I use beta readers to identify what should be deleted, revised or expounded upon in my content. If you know avid readers within your genre, then you may not have to pay for beta readers. Make sure to use a diverse group, as different views bring different aspects and more value to the review of your content. My beta reader group is made up of men and women of varying races and ages. Their only commonality, is they read within my genre often.

Once the flaws and flow have been identified, set about the work of identifying what suggestions are in keeping with your vision for your book and only change what you feel does not break the integrity of your vision.

Legally Speaking

Too many graphics and/or pictures in your book can drive up print costs. Even if you don't mind the increased print costs, there is still more to consider. Do NOT use pictures or illustrations you did not create without purchasing the right to use them or without express written permission to use them. In most cases, you will have to pay for the right to use copyright protected work. When investing in the right to use copyrighted material, make sure the rights of use that you have purchased match your intended use of the image, photo, or illustration. One way to get pictures to use for blogs and books is to Google "royalty free pictures" for a list of websites that contain royalty free images you can publish. Read the terms of use for these websites carefully. Consult with an attorney as needed.

At the time of publication of this book, my favorite site is **www.Pixabay.com** for royalty free pictures. Here are a couple of resource lists for more royalty free pictures:

- **http://blog.kozzi.com/design/25-free-stock-image-sites/**
- **http://www.digitalimagemagazine.com/featured-article/18-more-free-stock-photo-sites/**

Another free and legally worriless way to use pictures in your book is to take them yourself. If you take a picture, you own it and do not need further permissions to use it in print. However, be careful with what you take pictures of for use in publication. You cannot take a picture of others' art work, faces, original design, logos, and other recognizably unique works belonging to someone else without express permission.

Research, research, and more research. When

setting yourself up as an expert on a given topic, it is imperative that your information be correct and up-to-date. In non-fiction, you have to give credit to the originators of the facts that you use. Using statements and facts from another source could easily be plagiarism. *Plagiarism* is defined as committing literary theft by stealing or passing off the ideas or words of another as your own. Do not forget to site your sources; always give credit for someone else's original results, facts, figures, and work. Also be careful when using quotes from books or lyrics, those are also copyright protected.

In fiction you have to be cautious because most fiction is rooted in real life. There are three main areas of concern:

1. ***defamation*** (spoken injury/slander or written injury/libel to a living person or organization)
2. ***right of privacy*** (protection of individuals

from having private, embarrassing information published about them that is not "newsworthy" or of "public concern")

3. *right of publicity* (the right of living celebrities to protect their name, likeness or persona from being commercially exploited)

There are basically three classes of people that show up in fiction writing: non-celebrities, living celebrities, and dead celebrities. When writing about real people, keep in mind that anyone can take you to court for anything. However, just because someone feels they have been defamed, doesn't mean they actually were defamed. It is tough to prove defamation but the annoyance, and cost of going to court to defend yourself, may or may not feel worth a win in the end.

If you had no idea any of the aforementioned warnings were even necessary to get your vision to the world, this is all the more reason to get an attorney to review your book for legal holes that can cost you more than the legal consultation after publishing.

During your legal review, it is a great idea to speak with your attorney about whether the creation of a limited liability company (LLC) is necessary for your use of publishing your own books. If you plan to publish other people, you definitely need legal protection from the mistakes they will make in their writing that could cause lawsuits. But depending on what you will be doing with your self-publishing skills, there are other reasons an attorney will suggest incorporation. What kind of attorney do you need? My suggestion is that either an intellectual properties attorney and/or an entertainment law attorney. I recommend starting with the intellectual properties attorney. They are the ones that will help lower the risk of lawsuits being filed against you. An entertainment attorney knows the industry standards for things like contracts, events, etc... Sometimes the IP attorney may also be an entertainment attorney and vice versa. I propose starting off with an IP attorney and they will let you know if you need an entertainment attorney.

To Self-Edit Or Not to Self-Edit Is The Question

It is my stern advice that someone else should edit your work. If you are not good with punctuation, grammar, and spelling, then it is not just a bit of advice. Do NOT edit your own book. As a writer, it's hard to "kill your darlings" as Steven King says. The book in its entirety is a writer's baby. It's very hard to cut a finger, arm, or leg away from your own baby. When you're done, consider allowing a fresh set of eyes to edit your completed work.

For me, it is a must to have an editor. I have a tendency to see what is not there when I read my own work. Why? Because I know how it should read. I read with expectations that may not be fulfilled within the reality of my writing. Before giving my work to my editor, I do my own first round of revisions to submit a best draft copy. Everyone doesn't "clean before the maid comes to clean," so don't feel obligated to edit your work before paying someone to edit your work. I don't get too wrapped up in editing, I simply do a once over for a content check and I will correct or reword as I go but I only do this once and then let it fly to my editor.

In the submission email to my editor, I remind her of my usual faux paus: unmatched word tense, run-on sentences, switching between points of view, etc… With those reminders, I am less likely to have those mistakes overlooked. Editors, like writers, are not perfect; help them, help you have the best copy of your book possible.

Once the edits to your writing have been given back, much like with the critiques from your Beta

Readers, you then start identifying what edits are in keeping with your vision for your book. For example, to emphasize slang, I may have spelled a word phonetically instead of correctly. I meant to do this and I wouldn't change it even if the change was suggested by my editor.

Formatting Depends On the Format

Now this chapter heading sounds confusing, but it's the simple truth. You have to decide what format you will sell your book in before it can be formatted or typeset properly. For example, formatting a draft for print means there has to be extra margin space to the right of a left-hand page and to the left of a right-hand page. Why? Because the binding takes up space from the pages in the middle of the book and you want the margins to be even all around the portion of the page that is still visible to the reader as they flip from page to page. However, no extra margin space is needed for an ebook because no part of the page is impeded from view by binding. A specific consideration for ebook formatting is spacing, line returns, title fonts, picture positioning, etc... How these things look in your word processing document will NOT be the same when converted to an ebook format (usually an ePub, Mobi, or even PDF file).

Formatting is different from editing. Your final draft is taken as is (no more edits and no more corrections of any kind to the words themselves) and only spacing, margins, fonts and things of that nature will be changed to be accepted in the submission process for conversion.

Formatting is a service that I highly recommend an author outsource if they are impatient or easily frustrated. If you do not know the techniques accepted by the print-on-demand (POD) companies, you can cost yourself precious time. During the process, a poorly formatted draft can be submitted and re-submitted repeatedly before the preview is aligned well. Once the preview passes mustard, submission to publish can take a day or two before resulting in approval to go live and distribute to readers for purchase.

A Picture Is Worth A Thousand Words Or…

The next step is your cover art. Not that you are required to start it now. But that you are required to have it done by this step at the latest. Be sure to follow the guidelines for pictures that were included in the Legalities chapter of this book.

If you are not a graphic designer or creatively infused, do NOT work on your own cover art. A book cover is the first representation of your book. Any graphics on the cover should relate to the plot or the information therein. A huge cover mistake is having a book cover that is not represented well as a small thumbnail picture. All ebook covers should have a legible title and author name that can be easily read when displayed as a small picture. Book covers are often selected for purchase from a gallery of other mini book covers. Some print books are sold on websites and different online distributors in the same manner. Even if your book is being featured and not sold, there is a chance it could be displayed among other book covers as a thumbnail or have a small picture with text about your book beside it.

▲

Ever Heard of Bowker

An International Standard Book Number (ISBN) is like a social security number for your book. The number allows your book to be found with and by all distributors. Each format of your book needs a different ISBN assigned to it. This allows each format to have its own identity and therefore you will find the ebook when you are looking for the ebook version and the audio when you are looking for the audio version. Releasing a different version or edition to your book will require a new ISBN for each format you publish the new version/edition within.

Bowker is the official ISBN Agency for the United States. It is located in New Providence, New Jersey with additional operations in other parts of the world to make them truly international. Straight from their website (www.Bowker.com), they have "products and services that make books easier for people to discover, evaluate, order, and experience," making their services useful for readers and many aspects of the industry: publishers, authors and book distributors.

At the time of the publication of this book, you could go to www.Bowker.com and purchase one (1) ISBN for $125, ten (10) ISBNs for $295, and one hundred (100) ISBNs for $575. As you can see, the more numbers that are purchased, the less is paid per number.

You may also easily come to the conclusion from the increments that ISBNs are sold, that it is best to own a batch of them. Therefore if your intention is only to write one book or a few books, owning your ISBNs may not be economical. No problem, most POD distributors will assign one of their ISBNs to your book at no charge.

Why bother to purchase your own ISBNs? Having your own allows you to be registered as a publisher and appear in relevant publishing industry databases. These perks are especially important if you have started your own publishing company and want credibility within the publishing industry. Also if you will publish other authors' work, then the batches of ISBNs will be used up in a shorter period of time than if you were only publishing your own work.

The old system of ISBN assignments used a nine digit number. However, if you see a book with a nine digit ISBN that has been recently published it is probably because the numbers are purchased in batches and the publisher may not be finished using ISBNs purchased years ago and only assigned them just recently. The new system assigns a 13 digit

ISBN. All of my books follow the new digit system.

The barcode or Universal Product Code (UPC) on the back of books reflect the ISBN. Each printed book should have a barcode. Bowker.com will generate a barcode for you at an additional cost. If you are using a POD, a barcode may be assigned to your book for free whether you use their ISBN or use your own. If the POD you choose does not assign a barcode to your book cover for free, check out the following websites for a free one:

- www.bookow.com
- www.CreativIndieCovers.com
- www.TerryBurton.co.uk
- www.RacoIndustries.com
- www.Adazing.com
- www.Free-Barcode-Generator.net

Just for the sake of being clear, DO NOT REUSE ISBNS. The number only serves to point to one book in one format.

Of Course I Want To Be In The Library Of Congress

If I go through the trouble of writing a book and I actually accomplish my goal. You are darn tooting I want my book to be in the Library of Congress. That is the heaven of books in my country. And since this process doesn't add anything additional to your publishing costs, then it should be a no-brainer.

The Library of Congress uses what is called a Preassigned Control Number (PCN). The purpose of the number is to catalogue books going to publication that may be made available within libraries in the United States. Let's be realistic for a moment: a first book from an unknown author will likely not end up in a library. If you feel this way, then feel free to skip this step. However, if you are like me and you plan to keep writing books and one day be a well-known author, because you never gave up on your talent and you will push your way into other industries such as movies, television, broadway, etc... then also like me, you would like a PCN because you plan to be relevant enough to one day be in a library.

You have to apply for this number BEFORE publication. And it could very well hold up your publication process. For this reason, you may elect not to wait. I elected not to wait for this particular book as evidenced by the lack of a PCN on the title page. When I obtained my first PCN, it took a little less than two months to receive the actual number I was to have printed on my title page. On May 28th I went to http://www.loc.gov/publish/pcn/ and clicked the option to 'open an account.' Immediately, I was emailed a confirmation of my application. Later the same day, I was emailed instructions, an account number and a temporary password to complete the process. Please note that you will need your ISBN for the PCN process. That fact is why I have placed the PCN after the ISBN in the self-publication steps.

On the morning of July 31st, I was sent an email that contained my PCN. Within the email I was told to have the number printed in the exact way that it appeared in the email and to place that information on the title page of my book for publication.

To complete the process, I was given an address to send a published copy of my work and was warned that continued participation in the program was contingent on that last step as full compliance. I was also informed that sending a copy of my book to the Copyright Office does NOT satisfy the requirement. You will likely be given those same instructions.

Pick Five

I'm not incorrectly describing a lottery category (Pick-6 Lotto is the correct lottery category, in case you missed that reference and my attempt at a lame joke ☹), I'm speaking of the number of genres you can list for any one book on most distribution platforms. On the title page of your book, you are to list no more than five genres that categorize the content of your book. As an example, turn to the title page of this book.

There are two general genres: fiction and non-fiction. All other genres fit into either of these two genres. My idea of the basics for the two main genres are as follows:

FICTION (also a genre)

- comedy
- drama

- classic
- historical
- sci-fi
- horror
- mystery/thriller/suspense
- romance

NON-FICTION (also a genre)

- autobiographical
- biographical
- textbook/education
- self-help
- reference
- research/critique
- religious

Over the years we've seen the addition of several sub-genres, however they more or less fit under one of the categories above. The industry has even progressed to allowing the expanding of someone else's characters and work to be a genre. You can now take your favorite story, television show or movie and write a book that spins off the exact characters or picks up where the last known plot leaves off. This new genre is called 'fanfiction'.

For a true list of available genres for your book, research your distributor. Use the five genres that are available with your choice of POD company.

Another situation involving genres that is worth mentioning, is that some of these 'Amazon Best Seller' tricks are hinged upon you choosing odd, less populated genres available for selection on Amazon for print and ebooks. If you are considering using some of these techniques then keep the odder, less crowded genres in mind when selecting the genres in your POD profiles (not necessarily what is placed on your title page). What are these techniques? That's another book, of which I am sure several have been published. It is not my forte'. I am committed to sharing what I know firsthand and not speculation.

Theft Protection

Protection from others plagiarizing your work and being able to keep the proceeds comes in the form of a copyright for your book. If you have created the content within your book, not used anyone else's copyrighted work within your book without the proper recognitions and/or permissions, then you want to protect the original work as your own by copyrighting it.

With the United States being built upon and made better by the ideas and works of many people, it set about the business of protecting new ideas and works with registrations such as patents, trademarks and copyrights.

There is a myth that if you take your manuscript, mail it to yourself and leave it sealed after receiving it then it is admissible as evidence in a court of law as protection for the origination of your work. This is not the proper process to ensure protection for your work.

The correct process is fairly easy and it is quite affordable. For tips on the process, go to http://copyright.gov/eco/tips/ and for answers to frequently asked questions about the process, go to http://copyright.gov/eco/faq.html. You have two options for registering a single book. You can complete the entire process online or you can do it through the mail.

It is cheaper and quicker to do it online. Completion online is $35 and completion via the mail is $85. To register online, have accessible on your computer the completed book in an acceptable format to upload (*see* http://copyright.gov/eco/help-file-types.html) and a credit card with the funds available for your transaction amount.

When you are ready, go to www.copyright.gov/eco and select login. Although you may not have login credentials yet, there will be an option to register on the next page under the login boxes. You will fill out the application, pay the fee and upload a final copy of your book. Until you have completed all three steps, your application is NOT complete.

On the website the Copyright office states the e-filing/ online process generally takes three to four and one half months to complete. Please understand that your work will be reviewed for determination of whether it is copyrightable. However, when issued, the effective date of the registration will be dated for the date of application not the date it was approved.

When I received my official Certificate of

Registration for my first book, I was beyond proud. This was one of three major milestones for my first book; the first being when I actually finished my book and the other being when I actually had the first printed copy of my book in my hands.

On the certificate you are assigned a registration number, however it is not required that this number appear on the title page of your published book. In fact, years ago it was required that you have a copyright clause on the title page of your published book. However, that is no longer required although it is strongly suggested and still heavily in practice today.

Two Peas In A POD

The real saving grace of the self-publishing process is being able to use a print-on-demand (POD) distributor. This means you can upload your book to be available as a digital ebook copy and/or for readers to choose a printed copy that will be printed and delivered to them on a per order basis. What's great about this is gone are the days of having to buy a minimum quantity of printed books BEFORE they are available for sell in any capacity.

How does it work? I am a proponent of Amazon products. So I will tell you about selling your book on Amazon using www.CreateSpace.com for your printed book and using https://kdp.amazon.com/ for your ebook.

Both take special formatting (see the chapter on formatting for more information). Take your final formatted copy and upload it. The Amazon administrators will evaluate it on whether or not it is a good copy for publication. Among other things, they are checking for the resolution of your pictures, formatting blank pages, and sometimes even picks up misspelled words. You will get feedback on your submission within 24 to 48 hours. There may be required changes and/or suggested changes to make your end product the best it can be. They will not edit or review your work for possible legal problems (see prior chapters on both subjects for more information). Once submission has been determined to be the best submission by the Amazon administrators, you are a step closer to releasing your book for publication.

During the 24 to 48 hour approval waiting times, you should be completing your author and book information as a part of your POD account profile.

You will need information such as your author bio, your book summary and bank account information to receive payments in order to complete your profile. Another item you will need is pricing. Although every step thus far in this chapter has been for ebook and printed versions, it is my advice that you not set a price for your books until you know how much it will cost to print it through Amazon. Your ebook will be a straight percentage split between you, as author and Kindle, as distributor. Your printed book percentage is split between you and CreateSpace, after the printing cost is deducted. This means if your book is longer than average, your printing cost will be higher and therefore your book's retail price may need to be higher to meet your profit goal. Another consideration in pricing is the average cost of books in your genre that are within the same quantity range of pages and pictures as your book. A reader is not willing to pay more for your book just so that you can reach your profit margin. They want to pay standard pricing or even lower since you are a new author. Keep this in mind.

CreateSpace allows authors the option to purchase printed copies of their own book without paying retail price on Amazon.com. Within your CreateSpace account is an option to purchase your printed copies in any number, for a wholesale price based on printing costs. My book was a little over 100 pages and I was able to get a printed copy for less than $2.50. The more copies you purchase in one order, the lower your price per copy will be up to a cut-off. It is definitely cheaper per book to purchase 50 books than it is to purchase 1 book.

Why would you purchase copies of your own

book? There may be people or organizations you would like to gift your book, there may be events where you will need physical copies of your books for display or convenience of purchase by attendees.

Getting The Word Out

After your pool of family, friends, co-workers, church members, etc… have been exhausted, you will need a new pool of readers to purchase your book; assuming of course you wrote your book to make money from your work. The answer to finding new readers is marketing.

Worth repeating: social media is the great equalizer when it comes to marketing. Not only can you impact your word of mouth reach with your author platform (*see* that chapter at the beginning of the book), but you can now purchase affordable ads on Facebook and Twitter to name a couple of marketing opportunities using social media.

Another way to market on a budget is to get your book in the hands and the favor of an "influencer" in the field of your subject matter. An influencer is a person or group that has the ear of your target audience. For example, if your book is non-fiction then find influencers within the industry you have written about. If your book is fiction then one suggestion is to find respected/heavily followed reviewers within your genre to review your book.

Attend events where your target audience is present. Book fairs and festivals are great to find readers in general but also readers of fiction. Book clubs are a great focus for fiction marketing. There are many groups and associations focusing on your non-fiction topic that hold conferences, meetings, and other events you can attend, or apply to be a vendor during, to create a marketing opportunity.

What about virtual attendance? Now there are virtual book tours and tele-summits. Google such opportunities where you are paired with other authors or persons in your subject matter and you can share each other's fan base for exposure.

This is not the extent of the marketing available to you as a self-publisher but Google is your best friend. Search for ideas using wording like the following: cheap marketing ideas, free marketing ideas, marketing for indie authors, book marketing, social media marketing, and anything you can think of that will bring up even more search results.

Overwhelmed or you would rather spend your time within your talent of writing? There is a movement of social media marketers and marketers with author specific marketing plans for hire.

Budget Bonus

The first decision in the publishing budget process is what can you professionally do for yourself and what will have to be outsourced to other professionals. You are a writer. Unless you are using a ghost writer, writing is where your talent lies. Writers are not always good at all of the parts to the whole, when it comes to getting a book ready for publication. Know your strengths and your weaknesses for the betterment of your work.

Some of the information in this book is important enough to repeat within this chapter! I suggest that a writer should not edit their own work. If you are not good with punctuation, grammar, and spelling, then it is not just a suggestion. Do NOT edit your book.

It is said that to write, you must read. If you are

not an avid reader, do NOT publish your book without having a diverse selection of readers of your genre to read over your content (also see earlier chapter on Beta Readers for more detail).

If you are self-publishing and have never submitted a book to be printed or published digitally before, do NOT format your own book. Have you ever see an ebook or print book where the spacing, type set, and/or headings were "off"? You do NOT want those types of mistakes to riddle your book like bullet holes. Confused and distracted readers become brutally harsh critics when reviewing your book.

If you are not a graphic designer specializing in book covers, do NOT create on your own cover art. A book cover is the first representation of your book. As mentioned in detail earlier in this book, there are many things to consider that a novice would not know to implement in the creation of a proper book cover.

I read somewhere that the average book by an unknown author sells no more than about 250-300 copies, even if published by a well-known publishing house. That estimate can be with the help of a marketing department. If you would like to sell at least the average amount or over the average amount of copies, do NOT attempt to be your own marketing department. When your social media efforts have run dry, go ahead invest in a marketing expert to leverage your reach and increase the possibility of getting your book into more hands within your target audience.

There are industry prices for author services and there are prices ranged with the first time author/ independent self-publisher in mind. My passion and focus is the latter. I am not just a huge fan of self-publishing. I am definitely a fan of affordable services. If you too prefer professional yet affordable services for your self-publishing process, check out the a la carte services available at **www.AuthorSWCannon.com**

Let me blow your mind: at the time of publication, a self-publishing package on my website that included editing, formatting, and a book cover was available for around $1,000.

Author and Author Coach S. W. Cannon

S.W. Cannon was raised in Alabama but now lives in Georgia. Sha' (pronounced 'shaye') is a published author of both fiction and non-fiction.

She also has freelance experience in copy writing (fashion/style) and content writing (legal field) but her favorite work is within the lifestyle/relationship genre for both the male and female demographics. Add blogger to her credits, as she has a blog on relationships spanning topics for romantic and interpersonal relationships.

S.W. Cannon started helping other indie authors with writing and self-publishing. Her new found passion led her to lend her expertise to more authors with the writing and self-publishing process, so she became a coach.

Haven't written your book yet? You can do it. She can help: **www.AuthorSWCannon.com/Author-Coaching**

Made in the USA
San Bernardino, CA
17 February 2016